BATTLING THE BLACKOUT

by Charlie Ogden &
Sam Thompson

Minneapolis, Minnesota

Credits
Images are courtesy of Shutterstock.com. With thanks to Getty Images, Thinkstock Photo, and iStockphoto. Recurring images – mycteria, benchart, Andrii_Malysh, Bohdan Populov, Anastasiia Veretennikova, Francois Poirier. Cover – varuna, Anatolir, Myurenn, jakkapan, Zerbor. 4–5 – Leelaryonkul, hpphtns. 6–7 – TommyStockProject, Lia Koltyrina. 8–9 – Sergey Nivens, peterschreiber.media. 10–11 – Dylan Law, abstract_vector, Andrei Armiagov. 12–13 – Tim Cunningham11, iunewind, klyaksun, By Roobcio. 14–15 – Billion Photos, Janusz. Stepien, Seijen. zhengchengbao, DenisMArt. 16–17 – Vladimir Mulder, Dobra Kobra. 18–19 – Rocksweeper, Liuba Bilyk, Manbetta. 20–21 – AleksandraAv, showcake. 22–23 – Awe Inspiring Images, Ground Picture, Kinek00, Siarhei Kuranets. 24–25 – jaroslava V, Nejron Photo, Alenavlad. 26–27 – inavanhateren, Inked Pixels. 28–29 – Dmytro Balkhovitin, Diyana Dimitrova.

Bearport Publishing Company Product Development Team
President: Jen Jenson; Director of Product Development: Spencer Brinker; Managing Editor: Allison Juda; Associate Editor: Naomi Reich; Associate Editor: Tiana Tran; Art Director: Colin O'Dea; Designer: Elena Klinkner; Designer: Kayla Eggert; Product Development Assistant: Owen Hamlin

Library of Congress Cataloging-in-Publication Data is available at www.loc.gov or upon request from the publisher.

ISBN: 979-8-88916-591-0 (hardcover)
ISBN: 979-8-88916-596-5 (paperback)
ISBN: 979-8-88916-600-9 (ebook)

© 2024 BookLife Publishing
This edition is published by arrangement with BookLife Publishing.

North American adaptations © 2024 Bearport Publishing Company. All rights reserved. No part of this publication may be reproduced in whole or in part, stored in any retrieval system, or transmitted in any form or by any means, electronic, mechanical, photocopying, recording, or otherwise, without written permission from the publisher.

For more information, write to Bearport Publishing, 5357 Penn Avenue South, Minneapolis, MN 55419.

CONTENTS

Darkness 4
Why Did It Go Dark? 6
Get Reunited 10
What Could Go Wrong? 14
Laying Roots..................... 16
Your Survival Kit 20
Feeling Powerless 24
Switching On 26
The Disaster Checklist 30
Glossary......................... 31
Index 32
Read More....................... 32
Learn More Online............... 32

DARKNESS

How would you feel if all the lights went out? What if the TV went black?

If you are scared of the dark, be warned . . .

IT'S A WORLDWIDE BLACKOUT!

What should you do if the whole world loses power?

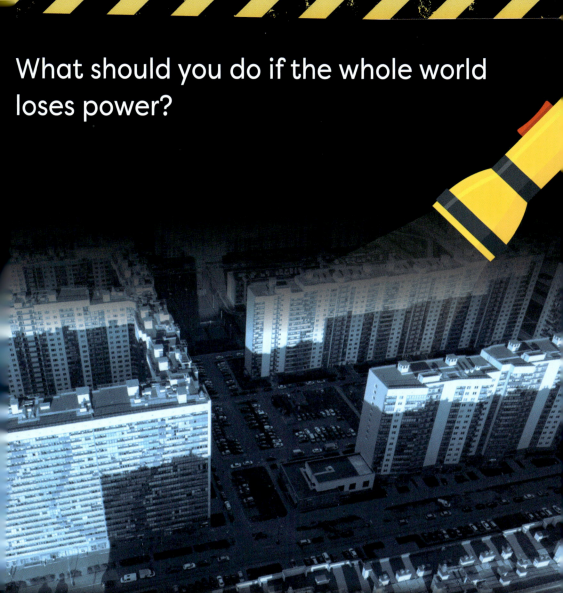

It is time to become a blackout survival **expert**.

WHY DID IT GO DARK?

What happened? There are many things that can turn off Earth's electricity.

An **EMP** is a burst of energy. It makes nearby electrical things stop working. Is a mad scientist trying to take over the world using an EMP?

Hopefully, there is no mad scientist. However, there is a chance nature has turned against you.

The sun can send out energy, a lot like an EMP. This is called a **solar flare**.

Solar flare

If it is not the sun, it might be a hacker. Someone may have broken into important computers.

The wrong hands on the right computers could put the world's electricity at risk.

What if the blackout was caused by a power **surge**?

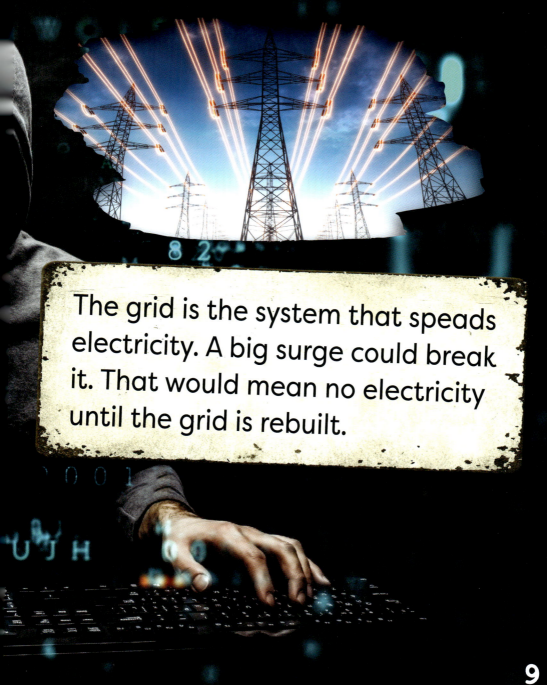

The grid is the system that speads electricity. A big surge could break it. That would mean no electricity until the grid is rebuilt.

GET REUNITED

No matter how the blackout happened, do you know what to do next? You'll need to find your family and friends.

Phone towers need electricity to connect calls. Wi-Fi doesn't work without electricity, either.

The only phones that may work are **satellite** phones. Satellites get power from the sun, not the grid.

Satellite

Still, you had better make those calls quickly. Once your phone battery runs out, there is no way to charge it!

What are other ways to **communicate**? A smoke signal may help people spot you.

Smoke signals are an old way of sending messages long distances. They use puffs of smoke that have meanings.

You can try leaving messages with whatever is around, too.

Help people trace your steps by leaving arrows on the ground. A few sticks should do it.

WHAT COULD GO WRONG?

Emergency services may not work if the power is gone. That means no police or firefighters.

Stay in pairs. Take turns sleeping at night. You may want someone keeping watch.

A fire can keep you warm and give you light. How can you be smart about making a fire?

Always build a fire inside a circle of rocks. This stops the fire from spreading. Keep water nearby, just in case.

LAYING ROOTS

Where will you stay if the blackout lasts a long time? You need food and supplies.

An old military base might work. But that could be hard to come by.

A farm is a good place to stay. Without power, all the stores may be closed. You may need to grow your food.

Maybe you can set up near a river. It has lots of water to drink. You could wash up in the river.

Firewood

Or try a forest. It has plenty of firewood.

It may be hard to tell what is out there in the dark. How can you keep yourself safe?

Set up a big fence around your space. Always make sure someone is keeping an eye out.

YOUR SURVIVAL KIT

A place to stay is important. But so are supplies.

You would need food that can last a long time. Gather pasta, rice, and canned foods.

The darkness may lead to accidents.

First aid kits are helpful in any emergency. Be sure to have bandages, cleaning wipes, and **medicine**.

You will need lots of batteries, too. Use them in flashlights and radios.

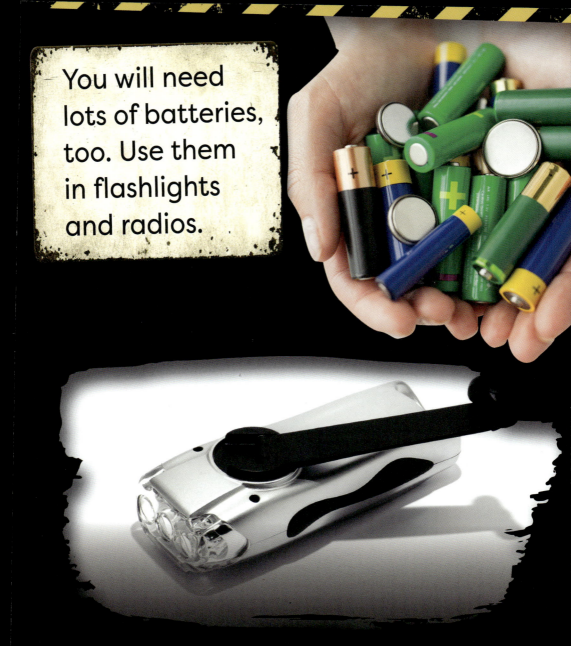

Try finding lights and radios that do not need batteries. Some can be wound up using a handle.

If you are really lucky, you may find a **generator**. These machines run on gas. They make electricity!

Generator

Gas

Generators and gas will be hard to come by. Be sure to use them wisely!

FEELNG POWERLESS

It may sound hard to live without electricity. But humans have been using electricity for only about 250 years.

Before then, people seemed to get by just fine without electricity.

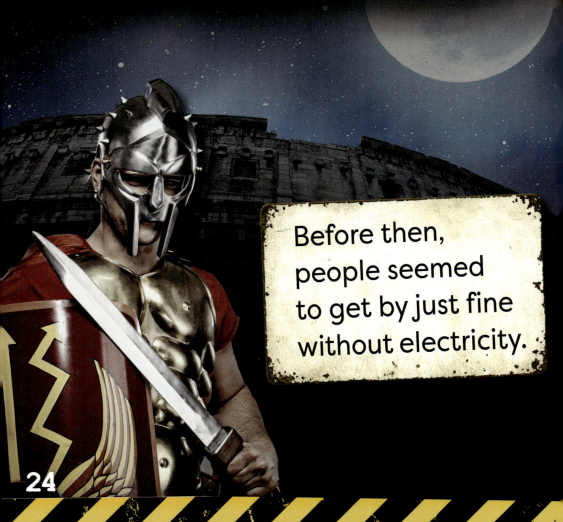

And remember, we built the electrical grid once. We can do it again if we need to.

In the meantime, think of all the new things you can try to fill your time. Learn to play an instrument!

SWITCHING ON

There are lots of ways to create power again.

If you are near a river, make a waterwheel. The flow of water pushes the wheel around.

That moving water makes power. With the right know-how, you might be able to make that into electricity.

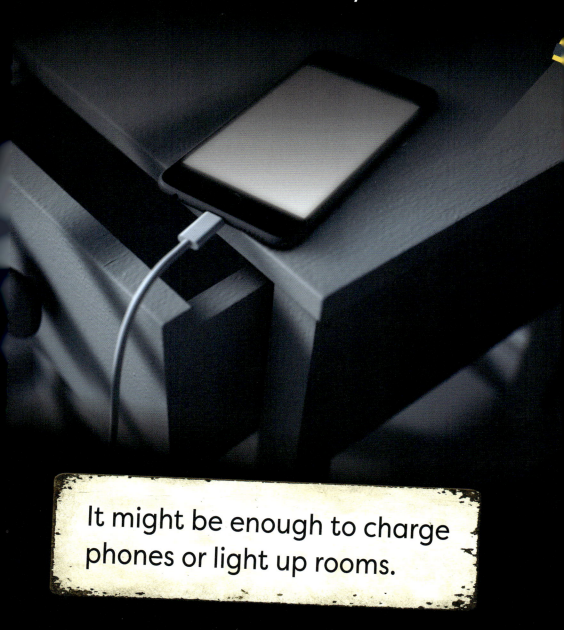

It might be enough to charge phones or light up rooms.

Windmills could help make food without electricity. They were first used to grind wheat into flour.

You may also be able to hook a generator up to them.

The biggest energy source we have is the sun. Solar panels can turn its energy into power.

If we all work together, we can get out of the blackout!

THE DISASTER CHECKLIST

How should you battle a blackout?

- ✓ Find out the cause of the blackout.
- ✓ Get with friends and family.
- ✓ Stay in pairs.
- ✓ Find a place to stay.
- ✓ Keep yourselves safe.
- ✓ Gather supplies.
- ✓ Make your own power.

GLOSSARY

communicate to share information, wants, needs, and feelings

emergency a sudden situation that must be dealt with immediately

EMP a pulse of extreme energy that may disrupt electricity

expert someone who knows a lot about a subject

generator a machine that creates electricity

medicine something used or taken to fight off sickness or pain

satellite a spacecraft that circles Earth and can be used for communication

solar flare a short, powerful explosion of energy from the surface of the sun

surge a sudden and very strong increase

INDEX

batteries 11, 22
fires 15
first aid kits 21
food 16–17, 20, 28
generators 23, 28
grids 9, 11, 25
phones 11, 27
power 5, 9, 11, 14, 17, 26–27, 29–30
rivers 18, 26
sun 7–8, 11, 29

READ MORE

Earley, Christina. *Electric Circuits (Physical Science).* Coral Springs, FL: Seahorse Publishing, 2022.

Mason, Jennifer. *Surviving in the Wild (Survival Stories).* Minneapolis: Kaleidoscope, 2020.

LEARN MORE ONLINE

1. Go to **www.factsurfer.com** or scan the QR code below.
2. Enter "**Battling Blackout**" into the search box.
3. Click on the cover of this book to see a list of websites.